THE
Archive Photographs
SERIES

CORBY

THE
Archive Photographs
SERIES

CORBY

Compiled by
Peter Hill

CHALFORD

The Chalford Publishing Company
St Mary's Mill, Chalford,
Stroud, Gloucestershire, GL6 8NX

ISBN 0 7524 0673 6

Typesetting and origination by
The Chalford Publishing Company
Printed in Great Britain by
Redwood Books, Trowbridge

Other books by the author

Local History

Corby At War
Rockingham Forest – Then and Now
In Search of the Green Man in Northamptonshire
A History of Great Oakley in Northamptonshire
Memories of Great Oakley
Portrait of Great Oakley

Literature

Sweet and Sour
Marianna
Travelines
Timepieces

Contents

Introduction

When I wrote the introductory chapter of *Corby: A Pictorial History* for the late Ron Sismey and helped him in the daunting task of choosing photographs for that successful book, it was immediately noticeable that one volume would not do justice to Corby – such was the wealth of illustrations of that town, whether commercial, industrial or, above all, of a personal nature. This is even more amazing considering that a great amount of archive material was lost in a disastrous fire in March 1979 that did irreparable damage to the former library building.

In this new book, as a result of intense public interest, a greater emphasis has been placed on old Corby village, and the people of Corby, the faces of whom will bring back memories and associations. Additionally, for the first time, the spotlight is focussed on the villages of the borough, with whom the town has been associated for many years.

It is difficult to imagine that the modern thriving industrial town of Corby was once an obscure Rockingham Forest village. However it was, and a fine one at that, with the right to hold a weekly market and two annual fairs from the time of Henry III. Its Royal Charter dates back to the reign of Elizabeth I and it exempted the men of the village from paying road and bridge tolls throughout the kingdom. One of the fairs, the unique Pole Fair, is still held, though now at twenty year intervals.

Throughout the ages, the area has proved popular with settlers. Bronze Age burials were discovered when the site of the ironstone works was being developed, Iron Age remains have been found around the Kingswood area and the Romans certainly made use of the rich ironstone deposits. The latter also used the fine local clay for pottery making, and kilns have been found off the Weldon Road. An important Roman road, the *Via Devana* (part of which is known as the Gartree Road), also passed through the southern area of the village, running from Huntingdon to Leicester. Sections of this were excavated in Southwood, Hazelwood and during the construction of the Beanfield Avenue-Cottingham Road underpass.

It is however the Vikings to whom we owe the name of Corby. When the invaders swept across the east of England in the eighth century a group, led by 'Kori', settled on the River Glen in Lincolnshire. Others moved on, perhaps via the River Welland, and settled in the vicinity of our old village, which became known as Kori-by, 'Kori's village'. A little of the Viking language and way of life also became part of the future Corby.

In Norman and medieval times Corby, as a Rockingham Forest village, had to behave itself, for the forest – an area (not necessarily woodland) set aside for hunting by the kings during their visits here – was placed under a set of special laws with a system of administration to safeguard these. Unlike some of the nearby villages, the men of Corby seldom appeared at the Forest courts for poaching deer or felling trees! There were also advantages of being a Forest village, such as virtually unlimited common rights – for grazing one's animals, or the use of fallen timber.

Village life went on quietly through the ages under a succession of lords of the manor: Braybroc, Latimer, Gryffyn, Hatton, Riche and finally the Brudenells of Deene (one of whom led the Charge of the Light Brigade during the Crimean War). Farming was the main occupation until the latter years of the seventeenth century, when weaving took over, occupying as much as ninety per cent of the workforce at one stage. The industry reached its height in the 1780s, but troubled times were to come to Corby. With the onset of the French Revolution, the Napoleonic Wars, a great agricultural depression in 1815, and land enclosure from 1829, it was hit hard by mass unemployment, poverty and starvation.

Years of misery continued throughout the century, until the coming of the railway in 1875, which required vast quantities of timber and bricks. Outsiders poured in to boost the village workforce. During the railway's construction, vast ironstone deposits were revealed on a scale the Romans would never have imagined. In 1880, a Birmingham industrialist, Samuel Lloyd, began ironstone quarrying here and later, in 1910, began the commercial production of iron. Stewarts & Lloyds (formed by amalgamation with a Scottish tubemaking firm in 1903) went from strength to strength. After Corby had been chosen, in November 1932, to be the site of one of the biggest iron and steel making complexes in the world with unlimited job prospects, an unprecedented invasion of workers began to take place, which was to transform it into a modern industrial town.

Strangely, Corby suffered little damage during the Second World War, and the post-war years saw another round of demand for housing as Corby, designated a new town under the 1946 New Towns Act, expanded further. The village of Great Oakley was incorporated in 1950, and in 1974, as a result of local government organisation, the villages of Stanion, Weldon, Gretton, Rockingham, East Carlton, Cottingham and Middleton were added.

The nationalisation of the iron and steel industry in July 1967, led to S & L becoming part of the newly-formed British Steel Corporation. But in 1979, following a Government White Paper, Corby found itself in a similarly disastrous situation to that it had experienced with the weaving industry slump in the previous century – the closure of the steel works. Mass redundancies took place and a general mood of despondency prevailed.

Yet the town refused to be beaten – it had bounced back before and would do so again. Hundreds of new jobs were created as other industrial companies came to Corby, among them the giant RS Components, ABR Foods, Oxford University Press and Weetabix. In 1995 it gained a major coup when Eurohub, Britain's first operational road and rail interchange, set up in the south east of the town; and the continental GEFCO car distribution group use Corby as a base at Barn Close.

Corby Borough now has a population of around 53,000, and the town continues to thrive. It has the geographical location and communications network, the resources, the people, the determination, and a belief in itself – a formula for success, that will carry it into, and beyond, the next century.

Peter Hill
August 1996

One
Corby

Wades Row, *c.* 1905. The present Station Road leads off to the right, and the High Street is in the background. This row of cottages, later renamed Davis Close, was almost joined to the White Hart and stood close to the railway track at the other end. They were demolished in the late 1950s, though the high bank in the foreground, leading up to the railway bridge, can still be seen today.

The White Hart, *c.* 1905. Back Way (now South Road) is on the right. Memories still linger of cows from nearby Page's Farm being marshalled down the High Street every Sunday morning during the 1930s. On one occasion, a cow made its way into the bar of the pub!

The White Hart, one of Corby's earliest surviving pubs, seen here in 1910. It was later demolished with the adjoining houses and replaced by the present building, which was built further back from the road.

William Dixon, landlord of The White Hart, with his family outside the pub, 1892. The pub was later run, until the First World War, by Mrs Florence Dixon, who is standing in the doorway.

Looking towards Station Road and Cottingham Road from the High Street in the 1920s. The house with the creepers in the row of buildings adjoining the White Hart is Vine Cottage, which is still standing today. Older villagers recall a kindly lady who lived there years later with many cats, and to whom strays would be taken to be given a home.

Corby, Kettering.

High Street, looking in the direction of the Jamb, c. 1900. On the opposite side of the road from the two men in the background, to the left of the low wall, was a set of steps leading to a row of four cottages known as Cock Row. Note the absence of any traffic – so different from today!

High Street, 1908. Note that the thatched roof and hedge of the house in the previous photo have been replaced by tiles and railings respectively. Note also the appearance of early street lighting, and a little traffic.

Bill Bishop, barber, outside his shop on the corner of the Jamb, in the 1920s. Older Corby residents can remember having a haircut here. The ladies' section was upstairs, reached via a spiral staircase, whilst the men were catered for on ground level where they got a very close 'short back and sides'. The large gates led to the back of Cock Row, and the gateway provided useful shelter to youngsters when it rained.

13

The Jamb, *c.* 1919, looking towards the bridge over the Willow Brook. The Cardigan Arms is silhouetted to the left of the picture, a general store with sunshade stands to the right, and the home of Mr Peerless, one of the village shoemakers, lies in the centre background. The name is pronounced 'jorm' and is believed to come either from the French 'jambe' meaning 'leg', or from an old word for an appendage. The block of stone near the centre of the picture was often used by children during their games and was later moved to a new home near the war memorial, where it can still be seen today.

The same scene in 1935 shortly after the celebrations of King George V's Silver Jubilee. The brick building where the crowd is standing was renamed Jubilee Building in honour of the occasion. The adjoining thatched building belonged to the Sarrington family, who had lived as bakers and grocers in the village since Victorian times. The small wooden building with lean-to roof in the centre of the picture, and the house behind it, belonged to the Payne family and were later destroyed by a fire. Note the star-like plate on the wall of the building to the left – the sign of the Northampton Brewing Company.

The Jamb, looking towards the High Street, *c.* 1919. A quiet, idyllic scene by the duckpond and bridge over Willow Brook. Bank House, the former home of the village benefactor, James Pain, stands in the High Street at the top of the picture.

The Jamb looking towards the High Street, *c.* 1894. Note the wide expanse of muddy track that was the main thoroughfare through the village, and the horse trough and yard of The Cardigan Arms to the right of the boy. Horse dealers conducted their business here for many years, until the outbreak of the First World War.

The bridge over the Willow Brook, *c.* 1900. This area is still prone to flooding today. The buildings at the top left of the picture are still standing, and were owned for many years by the Boon family, until 1985.

A later view of the Jamb in the 1920s. By now an extension had been added to the front of The Cardigan Arms, but the horse trough was still there. The building with the bay windows adjoining the pub housed a corner tea shop, a butchers and a general store.

Another view of the bridge from the Jamb. The road on the other side of the bridge was known as Dag Lane. The name also occurred in Cottingham, and possibly refers to the sheep which passed over here for centuries, 'dag' meaning 'wool matted with droppings', though the name could equally derive from the Viking word, 'dag' which means 'dew' but later came to refer to a mud-spattered track. The houses in the background to the left were known as Bishopgate, and have long been demolished, though some of their datestones may be seen today in the foyer of the Civic Centre. The early-eighteenth-century building on the right, at the corner of Tunwell Lane, was the home and workshop of Mr Peerless, the shoemaker.

The now-demolished Weslyan chapel in Chapel Lane, 1959. Services moved from the building to Corby Methodist church, Rockingham Road, which was opened in 1957 by Mr Simms, and it later became the labour exchange, with Mr Joey Spendlove in charge. The site is now a car park.

Rose Perrell (*née* Ward) and Annie Thompson (*née* Perrell) outside Weldon House, Tunwell Lane, in 1926. The building is now occupied by the manager of the Ex Servicemen's Club.

Tunwell Lane, looking at Tunwell Cottage and Weldon House, from Dixon's Farm, *c.* 1933. The street was originally known as Town Well Lane, because of the well sited in the vicinity.

18

Tunwell Lane. The thatched building to the left of the children shows The Old White Horse pub, the sign of which can just be seen. Next door to this was a farm where the Davis family lived for many years.

Tunwell Lane, looking towards Weldon House (far right), c. 1933. The house on the near left is West View, with the entrance to Stocks Lane on the opposite side of the road. Note the gasholder in the background.

Lloyds cinema, which stood near the corner of Lloyds Road and Rockingham Road (close to the old post office). It was originally an army hut from the First World War but was given by Stewarts and Lloyds to workers for recreational purposes, acting as a social centre and cinema until 1936 when the Odeon cinema was opened not far away. Another row of huts nearby provided accommodation for the workers.

High Street, 1920, with the Jamb leading off to the right of the boys. The alleyway to their left was known as The Jitty and this led to Back Way, one of two streets with that name in the village, the other being what is now Lloyds Road.

William 'Footy' Boon standing at the door of his shoemaking shop in the High Street, 1900. The grounds ran all the way down to Chapel Lane at the rear. A very talented man, 'Footy' had set up a shoemaking business originally in the Jamb, and was also bandmaster of Corby Brass Band (which later became Corby Silver Band, on the acquisition of new instruments), choirmaster of the Congregational church choir, and a parish councillor for thirty-five years.

'Thongers' at the rear of Mr Boon's shop, c. 1924. These young ladies were employed on stitching sandals. Only four faces can be identified: Rose Ward, standing in the centre of the middle row, with Miss Robinson and Miss Prentice to her right and in the back row, on the far right, Miss Bailey.

High Street, 1930s. All the buildings seen here are now gone and today in their place are a pet shop, glazier, chip shop and newsagents. The edge of the extant Co-op can be seen on the far left, as can the gates of the large private house, The Chestnuts, which is now St Andrews Walk.

Boon's shoeshop (shaded), left of the picture, and the post office, right, are now branches of a solicitor's firm. A cinema and shops were planned for the empty site, replacing a row of terraced houses. There was some controversy here, for, like a similar project further along the High Street, where Prentice Walk now stands (almost opposite the former Cock Row), the plan did not come to fruition. The picture was taken in the 1930s.

High Street, early 1900s. The building on the right was owned by the Chapman family for nearly 300 years. At the time of the photograph, it was a post office and stationers, but at one time it was involved in the manufacture of candles.

High Street, c. 1930, looking towards the old School House. The original Nag's Head is on the right, next to the Kettering Industrial Co-operative Society. Stocks Lane is on the left.

High Street, 1914, looking towards the Jamb end. The Nag's Head is on the left, with Stocks Lane on the right. Note the low wall between houses on the right of the picture. This later became Post Office Court and, walking through this short passageway today, you will see old barns and stables formerly belonging to the Chapman family, which were tastefully converted into homes in the 1930s.

Rear of the Nag's Head, c. 1919. The pub at this time was kept by William Atkins, and later by his wife, Alice, both of whom may be pictured here. This was at a time when many houses kept their own pigs and chickens, a fine clutch of which are strutting around the yard.

The Nag's Head in 1904. The landlord, standing to the left of the entrance, is John (Jack) Payne who kept the pub from 1898 until 1912. He then went on to run the nearby Black Horse pub with his wife, Ellen, until the mid 1920s.

Stocks Lane, 1925. Pictured left to right are: -?-, Walter Ward, Dick Perrell and Norman Bell.

Stocks Lane, 1922. Walter Ward in his back garden, with his dog, Gypsy, which he raced as 'Scarback'.

Meeting Lane, *c.* 1933. The gates of Rowlett School are to the left, with the old Congregational chapel and School House next door. The High Street can be glimpsed at the far end.

High Street, *c.* 1910. The School House of Rowlett School. This fine old building still stands, with a plaque in its garden wall commemorating the school (1834) which stood close by and was extended in 1881 by the renowned local architect, J. Alfred Gotch. The extension was in response to the increasing numbers of children attending from the villages surrounding Corby and the town itself which was transformed by the arrival of the railway and associated industries. The school was built by and named after a generous Corby benefactor, William Rowlett, who had prospered over the years as a wool merchant.

Meeting Lane, early 1930s. Perhaps no other picture so aptly depicts Corby old and new, rural and industrial. Here, domestic simplicity rubs shoulders with the iron and steel works in the background. The village was by then an expanding town, and would never be the same again.

Unveiling of the War Memorial, 1920. This is an interesting scene, since the flag is still draped over the memorial before unveiling – most photos show the memorial after unveiling.

High Street, looking from the Church Street end, *c.* 1949. The War Memorial is still outside the School House. It was moved in the early 1960s and placed close to the church, further along the street. Standing behind the beacon is the old thatched Barclays Bank building, with the Drury's Garage sign attached. It was built in 1609 and is still there today, a rare survival of old Corby, resisting the ravages of time – all its contemporaries have long since vanished.

Page's Farm (Church Farm), Church Street, *c.* 1930. Still standing, it was the home of Mr Davan Page who, as well as being a farmer, ran a taxi service for many years – an amazing feat for someone with only one hand!

Bert Ironmonger, shoemaker, who ran a business near The Nook. He is seen here seated outside his house. Something of a local character, legendary stories still abound about his involvement with poachers and adversaries.

There is something of a mystery about this late 1920s picture. A caption in a family album reads, 'Sunday Afternoon Snooze, The Nook' but the identity of the house and its occupants is unknown.

One of the surviving old houses in The Nook, 1959.

Church Street, *c.* 1910, in the direction of the parish church. At the time of this photo, this was still known as the High Street. The walls and gates to the old rectory are on the left. The ladies on the right are standing outside the gates of the Black Horse, considered to be the 'least notorious' of Corby's original five pubs. Like everything else in this photo, it has long since vanished and the scene is virtually unrecognisable today.

Church Street, late 1940s, looking towards the High Street, with the Black Horse on the far left.

Mr and Mrs Bradshaw, *c.* 1912, outside their house which stood nearly opposite the church. They ran a sweet shop much frequented by local children on their way to and from school. Mr Bradshaw was acknowledged as one of the most accomplished hedge layers in the area.

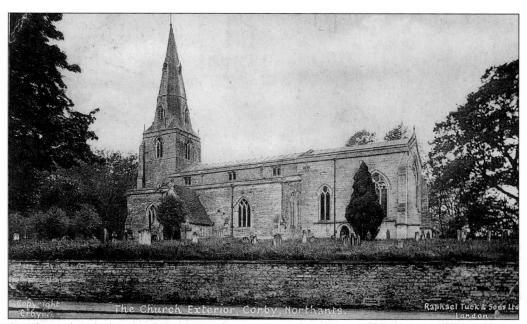

St John's church (originally St Peter's), *c.* 1910. It has several notable features including a scratch dial (an early sundial) and a very ancient, heavily eroded chest tomb (possibly of the Latimer family) in its grounds. There is a datestone from 1625 on the south porch wall.

Building workers, outside new brick houses being constructed in Weldon Road, *c.* 1908.

Some of the newly-completed houses and their occupants, *c.* 1908, in Weldon Road.

Weldon Road, looking towards the church, 1911, after building work had finished.

Weldon Road, looking towards the church, in the 1930s.

Weldon Road, as above, 1920s. It is difficult to visualise this scene today, because so much has changed. The buildings have all gone, except for a portion not in the picture (bottom left) near The Grove. The foreground is approximately where the roundabout now stands, and where the Oakley Road, Weldon Road (A427), Geddington Road (A6116) and Lloyds Road all meet.

Stanion Lane, now re-routed and named Geddington Road, c. 1920. The houses in the background are still standing while the thatched house in the foreground was destroyed by fire.

Corner of Stanion Lane and Weldon Road, 1935. This shows the house in the previous picture, belonging to the Crick and Patrick families, gutted by a fire, which also affected the adjoining house in Weldon Road.

Bridge in Stanion Lane, looking back towards Corby, 1930s.

The main Kettering Road at Oakley Hay, *c.* 1912. The inn in the background is the old Spread Eagle. Originally built in 1753, it became a coaching inn and toll house on the old turnpike road was known originally as The Eagle and Tower and was also temporarily called the New Inn, Oakley Inn and Cockayne Arms Inn. Locals however always referred to it as The Oakley Hay.

The same scene as the previous picture, *c.* 1920. The Kettering Road was replaced and diverted with the building of the present A6014 Corby-Kettering road in 1965. Today, the old road can still be seen, leading off to the left uphill just before the 'flyover', but heavily overgrown with weeds and grass.

The Corby Pole Fair, 19 May 1902. Celebrated every twenty years, this unique fair, began at dawn with the reading of the Charter granted by Elizabeth I in 1585 to the men of Corby, freeing them from road and bridge tolls in the kingdom. This was read at the entrances to the village: Station Road, The Jamb, Weldon Road, and Rockingham Road. Thereafter, anyone entering the village had to pay a toll. Those who refused were placed in the stocks. The third person from the left in the stocks is Mr Walker, who originally ran the Co-op. The lad grinning between him and the fourth 'rogue' is Pudgin Langley.

Outside James Pain's house, High Street, facing The Jamb, 1902. The banner reads 'Success to the Fête. Charter granted by HM Queen Elizabeth in 1575 and confirmed by H.M. King Charles II in 1682' (the correct date was 1670). The figure in the bowler hat, on the steps before his front door, is the Corby benefactor, James Pain, who gave a lot of employment to the town with his brickmaking and ironstone companies. The tickets given on payment of the toll can be seen attached to the hats of some of the men, though this did not guarantee exemption from a spell in the stocks!

Opposite: Pole Fair, 1902. Local dignitaries are being carried along the High Street to the stocks in Stocks Lane. Holding the charter is S. Willett, chairman of the parish council.

Pole Fair, 1902. Another group of unfortunates in the stocks at The Jamb. The pole which was used to carry male non-payers to the stocks was known as the 'stang', an old Norse word harking back to the days when the Vikings settled in the village. Wrongdoers in Viking society were carried round on a pole and pelted with objects. The word is still used today in Scandinavia.

Pole Fair, 1922. A huge crowd gathers to hear an extra reading of the Charter by the rector of Corby, the Rev T. G. Clarke, who is seen here at the War Memorial, to honour those who had fallen in the First World War. Corby Brass Band are providing the music. Also being chaired are the oldest villager, E. Chapman, and the chairman of the parish council.

Pole Fair, 1922. In the middle of the stocks can be seen the Rev T. G. Clarke, who also wore his distinctive mortar board at the 1902 Pole Fair. Note the box attached to the stocks for paying the toll.

Pole Fair, 1922. A concession was made to ladies – instead of 'riding the stang' they were borne on a chair to the stocks where they would have their hands, not feet, placed in the holes. The group are standing at the corner of Stocks Lane.

Pole Fair, 1922. Here, two more unfortunate ladies are being carried to the stocks. The man in uniform, holding a cornet, front right, is 'Footy' Boon, in one of his many roles – as the bandleader of Corby Brass Band.

Pole Fair, 1922. Queen Bess and her courtiers in the garden of the rectory. Local children dressed up and performed in a pageant, after which they were each given a pair of new shoes by the wife of the Rev T. G. Clarke. The festivities also included maypole and morris dancing.

Pole Fair, 1962. Rain affected the early part of the ceremony, but the weather improved as the day progressed.

Pole Fair, 1962. The fair had a modern flavour by now, with carnival floats and amusements in West Glebe Park and the streets. Here is Mr Dixon, and his son, in The Jamb, with a barrel organ on which sits a small dog (in place of the traditional monkey). The Cardigan Arms is in the background.

Corby Dandy Band, 1923. Little is known about this group of musicians who played at certain events in the 1920s, such as the Pole Fair. They are seen here on Empire Day, in the grounds of the rectory.

Empire Day, 1924, with members of the Davis and Rowlett families among the revellers posing for the camera outside Cardigan Farm in Tunwell Lane.

When ironstone quarrying began in earnest after 1880, the traditional occupation of farming maintained as important a place as ever. In this photo from around 1904, Corby farmworkers are haymaking. Among them is believed to be a member of the Ironmonger family. The cart has the inscription: 'S.M. Lathwaite, Corby'.

A Wilson belt conveyor and steam shovel in action, stripping ironstone for Lloyd's Ironstone Works, 1897.

A Whitaker combined excavator and double track skip transporter in action, c. 1909. The barrow men are wheeling top soil across the dump site, via narrow planks, the 'plank and barrow method', to enable the land to be restored for cultivation. The job was precarious – falls were a frequent occurrence.

Once the soil was removed, in two stages, the ironstone and sandstone were dealt with. Ironstone was broken up by explosives – the man on the left is holding shotfiring wires – and then loaded by hand into wagons which were horse-drawn along a three-foot gauge system. The tin shack at the top right of the picture was probably an explosives store.

Hand bearing' – ore being loaded into the wagons – at the 'Top Gretton' site, *c.* 1900.

A Wilson No. 2 long jib steam navvy, made by J. H. Wilson of Liverpool. This came to Corby in 1899, and was used to remove overburden where greater depths occurred.

A Grossmith excavator with a wheel conveyor, made by A. R. Grossmith, a Lloyds engineer. This picture, taken around 1909 at West Glebe, shows the excavator under erection. The gentleman in the waistcoat, on the right of the picture, was a well-known character called 'Bing Wilson'.

Another view of the excavator, now constructed, and at work at West Glebe, c. 1910.

In 1910, the first iron was made at Corby by the Lloyds Ironstone Company. The first furnace went into action in May of that year, joined by a second one in September.

A view of the two furnaces and the slag-crushing plant (behind, far right) from the Rockingham Road bridge, c. 1915. The Kettering-Manton railway line is on the left, with a private track leading to the works on the right. The signal box in the foreground also acted as a checker's station, to count the number of wagons passing through.

A group of Corby workers by the old No. 2 blast furnace stove, *c.* 1913. From left to right: George Rappy, Fred Hubbard, Jack Redshaw, Charley Langly, Billy Chapman and George Smith.

A fitting gang take a break by a furnace skip, late 1920s. Note the bottle of cold tea and wicker lunch basket – standard daily necessities.

An early ironstone 'saddletank' locomotive with Mr Bell, the driver, and George 'Turnip' Rowlett, as shunter, *c.* 1912.

Lloyds Ironstone Offices. These were situated close to the track near the Rockingham Road bridge (village side), and were later used by the Northamptonshire County Constabulary as the police station, before becoming the S & L Minerals Office. They were demolished in 1982.

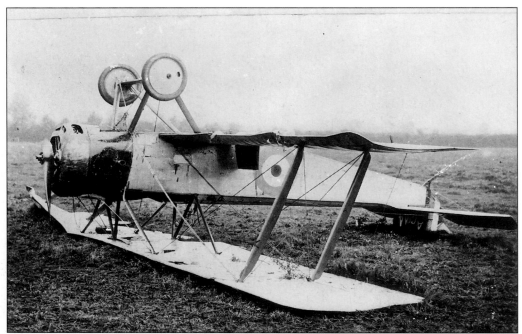

During the First World War, a Farman Shorthorn aircraft flew too low in the fog and crashed into telegraph wires at Pen Green Bridge. Here, in 1915, the plane has been disentangled.

'Crackers', 1917. Because of the First World War, manpower was short, so women went to work in the furnaces. Nicknamed 'crackers' because of the noise made when the slag pot was hit by their hammers, they include Miss Neal, Mrs Holland, Mrs Bailey, Emma Dunkley and Mrs Booth.

Because of the demands of the war effort, a third blast furnace was erected in 1917. This was the only new blast furnace built in Northamptonshire under the scheme sponsored by the Ministry of Munitions. The photo shows construction in progress.

Tipping iron ore and coal into calcination bays for loading into the blast furnaces, c. 1922. Below, two men are loading a handbarrow.

On the Glebe Farm site of the nascent iron and steel works, off the Weldon Road, symbols of rural and industrial life are seen here together: a haystack and to its right, a coke oven gas holder in the process of construction. The year is 1933, a turning point in Corby's history. Jack Lovelee, a member of the works staff, looks on at the scene.

North side of the furnaces, 1934. Corby was undergoing a period of development on a scale never seen before, as the existing Lloyds Blast Furnace Plant was being reconstructed as part of a scheme to create the biggest and most modern iron and steelworks in Europe. A new water header tank stands in the centre, amidst construction work.

The first 5360 R & R digger to be built at Corby quarries (Short Leas), c. 1936. Deeper excavation was necessary in order to obtain greater quantities of iron ore.

A service pipe erection team, 1930s. They are standing in the area where hot metal is off-loaded when it arrives from the blast furnaces to be deposited into mixers. One of the workers is holding a chain for lifting service pipes. The chargehand, Albert Burton, is on the right. A Bessemer boiler house stands in the background.

Three blast furnaces in action, viewed from the front side, mid 1930s.

Increased demand and production led to a fourth furnace being built by E. N. Wright of Wolverhampton. Here it is shown almost completed; it was first lit in June 1937.

With the outbreak of the Second World War in 1939, German managers and engineers at the works had to leave. Preparations for camouflaging began, ranging from smoke screen generators being sited around the streets of Corby to block out the glare from the works at night, to the painting of buildings in certain colours. Here poles are being erected to create an enclosed tunnel. Strangely enough, although a prime target for the enemy, the works were hardly touched and few houses were damaged. A bomb blast from an air raid prematurely opened the new post office nearby, which was due to open officially the next day!

Corby Home Guard, outside the tube works, *c.* 1942. On 14 May, Sir Anthony Eden asked for volunteers between the ages of fifteen to sixty-five to combat possible German parachute landings. 1,300,000 people responded and the Local Defence Volunteers were formed, later to become the Home Guard. Different sections of the works formed their own companies. Among the faces are believed to be Alec Coldwell and Sam Muir. On the extreme left is John Glen who was chief metallurgist at the time.

The giant bucket of a Baring digger can be seen here, rearing up like a dinosaur, after a blast at a Corby quarry in 1948.

W. Garnett rock drilling for Stewarts and Lloyds, in 1948.

An aerial ropeway for transporting ore from Desborough pit to the works at Corby. This was a special grade of ore used to mix with that found around Corby.

One of two headless skeletons found near the site of Roman remains which was discovered whilst quarrying at Priors Hall in 1953. The whole area is very rich in Roman remains and, at nearby Bulwick, ironstone working during that era was on a vast scale – comparable with that at the Forest of Dean.

At the same site at Priors Hall, a tessellated pavement was found, followed, in September of the same year, by the discovery of these floor piers which supported the floor for a Roman heating system, indicating a building of some importance.

View of the gas cleaning plant, the four blast furnaces, and beyond these, the Rockingham Road Schools, Pen Green Estate, and recreation club. Standing on the roof of a 193ft high gas holder is Robert Binley, fuel technician (right), talking with a reporter in 1948.

Two boys, sitting on the Rockingham Road bridge, watch the trains at the works in the 1950s. Note the blast furnaces standing in the background.

A W1400 dragline working in a gullet at Cowthick quarry in 1967. To the left is hill and dale, restored land, and on the far left plantations. The huge 'walking draglines' were a noticeable feature of the Corby area for many years.

Removing large sandstone slabs after reclaiming the land, using either fourteen pound hammers, or by blasting. Eric Grey and Andy Addison are shown on one of the massive slabs.

A general view of Priors Hall showing stripping, drilling and loading in operation in 1968.

Forestry was also an important occupation in Corby. Pictured are members of the S & L Forestry Department. The back row includes: Eric Grey, Ernie Scarrat, John Brookes, Charlie Rust, Tetric Outon. The front row includes: Dick Wallace, David Coleman and Cecil Kerfoot, foreman.

Making pit props and larch fencing at the woodyard off the Kettering-Weldon road.

A dragline at work at Barn Close quarry. The tube works can be seen in the background.

Sometimes work necessitated the removal of certain buildings. Hollow Bottom Farm is shown in 1957, before demolition, with a 1150B walking dragline in the background.

The front wing of the research department of Stewarts and Lloyds after it was gutted by fire in 1968. Many still remember the incident.

A Barclay steam locomotive used around the works for many years. The locomotives were overhauled or repaired at the main engineering shops. One of these can be seen at nearby East Carlton countryside park today, along with other relics of Corby's iron and steel era.

Another picture of a Barclay locomotive, this time in motion in the 1960s. They were painted bright yellow so as to be easily visible.

The works from the Rockingham Road bridge. A large British railways engine can be seen in the foreground, with a Barclay locomotive in the background. Also visible are the blast furnaces, gas cleaning plant, water tower, waste gas blasters and coke oven chimney stacks.

Dragline buckets were gigantic. It is said that, in some cases, a double-decker bus could fit into one – certainly a rugby team could! Standing in the bucket of the more modest W1400 is a young Ron Sismey (left), who later formed the Weldon Local History Society.

George Binley's 'gang', who built the giant W1800 walking dragline between 1960 and 1963. This was the largest of its kind, weighing nearly 2,000 metric tons, and worked at the Great Oakley quarry.

The W1800 began working in autumn 1964, and is seen here at work in the vicinity of where the Safeway supermarket now stands. Local people would watch in fascination whilst it was in operation. Quarrying continued until January 1980, and the dragline was finally dismantled in 1983.

Outside the Minerals Estates Workshops, Shire Cottage, Rockingham Road. The men were responsible for fencing, plantations, and drain laying. The cottage is still there, with its datestone of 1851.

Priors Hall golf course. This was opened to the public in the summer of 1964. The results of earlier quarrying activity in the vicinity can be seen in the foreground.

The new Deene coking plant at the steel works marked the completion of the first stage in the coke oven development programme. The ceremony of lighting-up the coke ovens is shown here in September 1961.

The presentation of long-service certificates to S & L employees, 1969. Pictured left to right are: George Todd (42 years), Len Davis (36 years), Walter Mayes (48 years), William Land (32 years) and John Mason (33 years). These men had served for a total of 191 years between them.

From the following year, gold watches instead of certificates were presented for long service. The presentation here was at Brigstock Manor, July 1970.

The works first aid competition winners, 1962. Holding the trophies (the Shield and Hewitt Cup) are, left to right: G. Mason, J. Spriggs, A. Mallet, J. Moffat, A. Aldwincle, R. Willock, G. Guest, L. Pringle, C. Webb, N. Tranter, C. Tomblin and G. Mason.

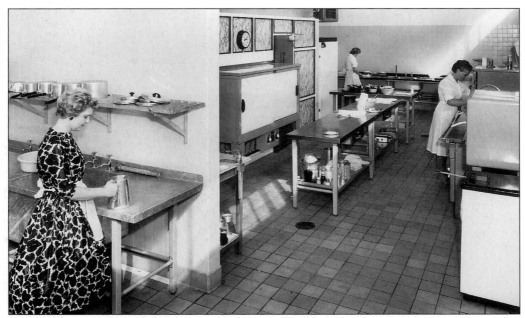

The kitchen of the new Stewarts and Lloyd students hall, which was opened in Corby, September 1961.

The end of an era. Gradual demolition of the steel works began in August 1980. Here the tall sinter chimney comes down, watched by two local spectators.

Constuction of Kelvin Grove, 1934. Though Corby village had been transformed and expanded by the coming of the railway, brickmaking and ironstone workings in the late 1800s, full-scale house construction did not take place until 1933, when the new steel works opened. Waves of workers poured in, especially from Scotland, and made Corby their home.

This view in 1934 shows the early development of both the works site and land for housing. Occupation Lane, in the foreground, soon to become Occupation Road, is houseless except for Occupation (Pears) Farm, where a water tower stands today.

Kelvin Grove, newly completed in 1935. Among the new residents is Bill Lorimer, shown here sitting on the bicycle.

The Odeon cinema building, Stephenson Way, corner of Rockingham Road, 1949. The row of shops included that of Johnnie Murdoch, newsagent and tobacconist.

Inside Johnnie Murdoch's shop, 1951.

Rockingham Road shops, looking towards the cinema and railway bridge, 1934.

Rockingham Road shops from the opposite direction to the previous picture, 1949. The double doors of the 'new' fire station can be seen to the left of the cyclists, and on the corner is Tipaldi's cafe. This was a popular haunt, especially during the war, since it had one of the first espresso coffee machines in England, and a gramophone for playing music to the customers.

Lloyd Cottages, 1951. These were later nicknamed 'The Black Houses', because the outer walls had been sprayed with tar, after residents had complained about dampness. They stood along Lloyds Road close to where the new fire station now stands.

At the other (village) end of the town, 1934. The new housing of Bessemer Grove can be seen in the foreground.

Building at the junction of Rockingham Road and Willowbrook Road, 1951.

Whitworth Avenue, 1950s. The blast furnaces can be seen in the background.

Occupation Road, 1950s. Except for the being able to play in the road at this time, little has changed.

Rockingham Road, looking towards Rockingham, 1940. Tom Kirkham's farmhouse stands on the left, the only building for a considerable distance.

An interesting view of the Rockingham Road area, April 1936. The welfare club and playing fields are in the centre of the picture. Occupation Lane to the rear of the building is undeveloped and the Rockingham Road shops and Corby Hotel are unfinished. Note the Samuel Lloyd School, top left, and the haystack at West Glebe, far right.

Stephenson Way and Telford Way, 1951, with the blast furnaces in the background.

Stephenson Way, 1951. Taken from the flats of the Odeon building.

The new Corby town centre, 1958. There are no roundabouts or pedestrian crossings in George Street, which winds to the left of the photo. The shopping centre can be seen to the right of the proposed civic centre site. The entrance to Studfall Avenue can be seen top left.

Corporation Street, looking towards the police station, 1959. The post office, which later moved to Post Office Square, is on the right, by Spencer Court. The street here has a similar appearance in design to George Street, but is now pedestrianised and partly-covered.

Willowbrook Road shops, 1959.

The British Steel conference centre, off Cottingham Road, 1950s. The building is now the base of the British Institute of Management.

The old bridge at the bottom of The Jamb, looking north, early 1930s. This scene would soon completely change as many of the old houses made way for new developments. Crossing the bridge are Irene Davis and Vera Bailey.

Caldermeadow Lodge, 1960s. As Corby spread outwards, it was inevitable that other old landmarks would disappear. This Victorian farmhouse, on the edge of Kingswood, which had been part of the Great Oakley Estate for many years, was a casualty. The last occupants were Mr and Mrs George Bates, who later moved to Woodlands Farm in Great Oakley. Bungalows now occupy the site, which lies almost opposite Kingswood School.

Keeper's Lodge, 1950. This was another casualty when the Kingswood Estate was built. It was also known as Kingswood Lodge and in the nineteenth century was the home of the Great Oakley Estate gamekeepers, many of whom were members of the Patrick family. Pictured are Mr and Mrs Bob Taylor, the last occupants. It stood in Patrick Road, near the telephone exchange and almost opposite the Safeway supermarket.

An aerial view of the Weldon Road part of the works, 1968. The office block still exists and there are traffic signals today at this junction. The neon-lit 'Stewarts and Lloyds Limited' sign, behind the block, will bring back memories for many.

Corby Iron and Steel Works in its heyday. The extent of the area's development, both industrial and domestic, is captured in this 1970 photograph.

Another aerial view of the works in the 1960s, with Lloyds Road in the foreground, the village bottom right and the old post office, on Rockingham Road, bottom left. Today the site of the works area on the left and centre is the site of the Asda supermarket, shops, offices and other industries.

An aerial view from the late 1960s. St John's church and the village are at the bottom of the picture, with the roundabout where the Weldon, Lloyds, Oakley and Geddington Roads meet.

Corby Council Schools' May Day, 1931.

The Corby church Mothers Union outside the rectory, 1930.

The Clayholes. Originally part of the James Pain Brickworks, they became filled with water and acted as a popular, if dangerous, play and swimming area for local people, especially in the inter-war years. Today they are sealed off on the St James industrial estate site.

Corby people at the Clayholes, late 1940s. Four men pose for the camera whilst another group of people, in the background, prepare for swimming at the water's edge.

Bus service to Glasgow, outside St Andrew's church in Occupation Road in the 1950s. Because of the large Scottish population in the town, it was only natural that visits to and from Scotland would be popular. This service was operated by Mr Hinds.

Mothers' Union outing, *c.* 1955. The group is standing outside The Cardigan Arms in The Jamb. From left to right are: Mrs Tyrell, Mrs Binley, Mrs Elsie Goode, Mrs Shillaker, Mrs Simmons, Mrs Rowlatt, the driver, Mrs Hargraves, Mrs Ironmonger, Mrs Jessie Marshall, -?-, Mrs Hudson, -?-, -?-, -?-, -?-, Mrs Brooke Westcott, Mrs Bell and Mrs Incles.

Sarrington's grocery store, 1950s. Maurice Sarrington, the owner, is pictured with two of his assistants. The family were active in Corby business since the 1800s. The shop still stands at the corner of The Jamb and High Street, although it is no longer in the hands of the family.

On 4 March 1943, King George VI and the Queen visited Corby for a tour of the works. They are seen here, welcomed by a large crowd, on their arrival from the station.

The King and Queen inspecting the works, with the chairman of Stewarts and Lloyds, Allan Macdiarmid, behind them.

Corby Adult School football team, 1920: Kettering and district Sunday School league. Back row, left to right: Mick Brannon, George Redshaw, Percy Bell, Reg Atkins, Jim Perrell, Fred Chambers. Middle row, left to right: Bert Dixon, Albert Smith, Cecil Clark. Front row, left to right: George Lattimore, Arthur Dixon, John Nicholls, Archie Dixon, Dick Perrell.

Corby United football team, 1930. Back row, left to right: Bert Dicks, ? Bates, ? Marshall, Dick Perrell (goalkeeper), Tom Burdett, Harry Pullen and George Edwards. Middle row, left to right: Eric Streather, ? Graham, ? Walker. Front row, left to right: Will Palliser, ? Rowlett, Arthur Dixon, ? Mears and ? Marshall.

Teachers at Rowlett School, early 1930s. Back row, left to right: Miss Bottom, Mr Poskitt, Miss Barton. Front row, left to right: Miss Huffer, Miss Chapman, Mr Arthur Brooks (headmaster), Miss Cottingham. Miss Chapman was a member of the family who ran the post office for many years in the High Street. She was a talented musician and one of the most popular teachers Corby has ever known. Pupils were always interested in what brooches or necklaces she was wearing and would follow her around everywhere.

Empire Day, Rowlett School, June 1917. Back row, left to right: Ivy Wells, Jessie Andrews, Miss Dicey, Jessie Bailey, Clive Payne, Eva Green, May Beadsworth, Mr Brooks, Ivy Dunford, Ada Boon. Middle row, left to right: Gordon Underwood, Arthur Perrell, Clive Ivett, James Cottingham, Horace Gray. Front row, left to right: Len Brooks, Eric Streather, Ted Lattimore.

May Queen crowning ceremony and Empire Day celebrations, Rowlett School, 1925. The May Queen is Hilda Beadsworth. Her maids of honour (wearing chaplets of flowers) are Florrie Plowman, Muriel Walker, Ruby Miller and Laura Battams. The little girl, sitting at the front of the platform, is Iris Langley. After the occasion Mrs Sarrington, who crowned the Queen, gave everyone on the platform presents including beads, bottles of scent and a shilling.

Rowlett School choir, 1928. The pupils proudly display the shield they have won at the Oundle Music Festival. The headmaster, sitting in the middle row, is Albert Brooks.

Corby fire officers in the 1920s, at the original Rockingham Road fire station opposite the old post office building. This was later moved further along the road, among the newly-built shops. Back row, left to right: W. March (fire chief), W. Fellows, W. Driver, H. Madden. Front row, left to right: Tom Goode (who later became fire chief and was awarded the MBE), Dick Perrell.

Winners of the Blackpool festival of drama, March 1948. The Corby team performed a piece named 'The Apple Tree'. Back row, left to right: Margrete Cory, Mr Gillan, Anne Clarke, Kathy Laird, Miss Palmer, Carol Howell. Front row, left to right: Betty Vint, Margaret Vint, Isabel McEwan.

Samuel Lloyd School for Girls hockey team, 1950/1.

Prefects at Rowlett Road School, 1951.

Modelling self-made clothes for the Samuel Loyd School speech day, mid 1950s.

Two

Corby Borough Villages

Great Oakley: the bridge over Harpers Brook, *c.* 1900. This area of the village was known as 'Duckpaddle'. Unfortunately the trees in the foreground have long since gone, and the old stone bridge, which replaced a ford in the eighteenth century, gave way to a modern concrete structure in the late 1960s.

Great Oakley: the old village store, *c.* 1903. This was in the area of the village known as 'The Other End', now Woodlands Lane. The shopkeeper, Louisa Allsopp, is shown with her daughter, Gladys. The post office was next door. The house is still there, but the thatched roof has gone.

Great Oakley: the old village school in 1900. It was built in 1867 for thirty-five pupils by Sir William de Capell Brooke, lord of the manor, and closed in 1957. Note the appearance of Brooke Road, known at the time as 'The Street'.

Great Oakley: inside the school, 1938. Members of the Smith, Payne and Pears families can be seen among the faces. The school was one room with a curtain dividing the younger pupils from the older ones. On leaving, most of the pupils would go to Samuel Lloyd School in Corby.

Great Oakley: a rare print of the village church, St Michael and All Angels, from around 1750. The original part of the church was built in the thirteenth century, and there are relics from Pipewell Abbey which was dissolved on 5 November 1538. Until that time, monks from the abbey would walk to the village to take services in the church.

Great Oakley: May Day procession in Oakley Park, 1942.

Great Oakley: Park Cottages, 1920s. The house was something of an attraction to visitors, with its fine clematis formation trailing around the wall with the words 'Home Sweet Home' and the initials FHD which were those of its creator, Francis Henry Dickson, who was a gardener at Oakley Hall. Mrs Annie Dickson is standing on the doorstep.

Great Oakley: The Other End (Woodlands Lane), *c.* 1900. This idyllic scene is virtually the same today, except that slate tiles have replaced the thatch.

Oakley Hay: Charlie 'Nibby' Bradshaw riding his Penny Farthing bicycle past The Spread Eagle, *c.* 1937. He was the village chimney sweep and woodsman, and was a popular figure in the area, often seen riding the bicycle in Corby and around the district.

Rockingham: looking up the main street towards the castle, c. 1890. The boys are sitting around the base of the old Market Cross. In 1894, a memorial pillar was added to this, in memory of Laura Maria Watson, a member of the family who still own the castle. In the foreground is a post boy in uniform.

Rockingham: almost the same scene in the previous picture, but the date is now 1904, and the addition to the Market Cross can be seen. Members of the Leicestershire Archæological Society can be seen about to leave the village for Stamford station, after lunch at the Sondes Arms and a visit to the castle.

Rockingham: outside the Sondes Arms, 1925. The pub can be traced back to 1663, when the village was rebuilt after the Civil War. The landlady, Mrs Hunt, is on the left. On her right is May Manton (later June Burton), who became a Leicestershire beauty queen, and later moved to Corby where she ran a business, initially in Rockingham Road.

Rockingham Castle, c. 1925. This has changed little in appearance over the years, and is a popular tourist attraction in the area, giving magnificent views over the Welland Valley and beyond. Besides its strategic importance, it was the chief centre for the administration of Royal Forest Law in Rockingham Forest for centuries. It passed from the Crown in 1544 into the hands the Watson family, descendants of whom still live there.

Rockingham fire brigade, 1930s. The 'engine' was kept at the Top Lodge of the castle but was far from any water source. Fortunately it was never used. Left to right: Henry Woods (carpenter), Jack Jarvis, Stanley Dowsing, Sid Masters (gamekeeper), Bill Miles, Jim Woolley, Wally Spriggs, Arthur Perrin, Charles Mears (seated), Bill Mears.

Rockingham Hill: one of a group of wagons taking the children of Cottingham Methodist chapel on their annual outing, 1929. The outing was always to the same destination, using the same route from Cottingham to the Lodge gates at the top of Rockingham Hill where 'sprags' (a kind of braking device) were attached to the wheels before the descent. Passing through the village they would go on to Caldecott, turn round and return via Great Easton to Cottingham for a tea party at the chapel.

Cottingham: Corby Road, looking towards the village and 'The Cross', *c*. 1910. The view to the left at this point is still magnificent, with the church nestling among the trees below.

Cottingham: well head at the corner of Corby Road and Rockingham Road, *c*. 1920. Cottingham with its adjoining sister village, Middleton, was always blessed with a plentiful water supply, and relics of this in the form of springs and old pumps can be seen everywhere. The main water supply came from the well pictured here which has long been filled in. The plaque was inscribed 'Erected by the copyholders, 1854, William Thorpe, John Spriggs, Bailiffs.'

Cottingham: washing day in School Lane (formerly Dag Lane), 1928. Members of the Jolley family are doing the Monday wash, with buckets of water from the nearby well. These were the days before mains water.

Cottingham: Church Street, looking towards the High Street, c. 1910. The grocer's shop on the left was also at one time a post office and an undertaker's. Together with the adjoining archway building, it is now a craft studio and workshops.

Cottingham: the old Spread Eagle in the High Street, *c.* 1912. This was one of five pubs that used to be in the village.

Cottingham: The Spread Eagle in the mid 1960s before being rebuilt. The adjoining portion seen in the previous photo has already been demolished.

Middleton: Main Street, looking towards Cottingham, *c.* 1912. The street has hardly changed in appearance. Once again, note the use of buckets. One of the houses on the right hand side (out of view) has a plaque from Victorian times calling the road 'Birmingham Street'. The village gets its name from its location between Cottingham and East Carlton.

Middleton: looking towards The Hill, *c.* 1905. The entrance to the old Red Lion pub is out of view on the left. Another well head (1844) with a spring gushing water is still visible today, up the hill on the right, adjoining the walls of what is now East Carlton Park.

Stanion: High Street with the old Cardigan Arms on the left, *c.* 1910. The church was renowned for the whalebone that can still be seen inside and was said to have been a rib belonging to the legendary giant Dun Cow that gave milk to the whole village!

Stanion: tug-of-war champions, *c.* 1930.

Stanion: Battle Bridge, over Harpers Brook, *c.* 1910. This can still be found, rebuilt in the same form, on the footpath to Brigstock, behind the new Village Hall.

Stanion: Coronation Day (George VI), 1937. In the old school yard, Mr David Gray, well into his eighties, and the oldest inhabitant in the village, presents mugs to the children, whilst his son, Joe, looks on. Among the children are members of the Buckle family and Lilian Pick, dressed as Britannia.

Stanion: May Day procession, outside the village school, 1925. Note the pushchair, in the foreground, decorated and garlanded with evergreens.

Stanion: The Wash Brook, with Willow Lane and Skinner's Farm in the background, c. 1910.

Weldon: East Bridge on the Oundle Road with Church Street (formerly Back Street) on the left, looking towards the village, c. 1912.

Weldon: Church Walk, c. 1918. The thatched house is now demolished.

Weldon: The Cross, *c.* 1920. The old King's Arms, a former coaching inn, stands on the left and the narrow entrance to Bridge Street (formerly Taylor's Hill) virtually a track, is by the side of the off-licence opposite. The pub was demolished in 1962, along with a few cottages, in order to widen the street for vehicular access, and was rebuilt further back in its present form. The house on the corner of Bridge Street has also been demolished, and even today the street is still quite narrow – one wonders how traffic managed to negotiate this stretch in the past.

Weldon: one of the former butcher's shops which stood close to the George in Stamford Road (locally known as Deene Road), 1921. Included in the picture are Bill Mace, on the left, Brock Prentice, Mrs Payne, Rose Waterfield and Fred Payne. The shop is well-stocked, with a good display for Christmas trade.

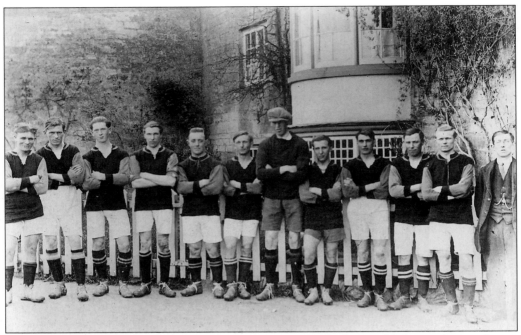

Weldon: Weldon Football Club, outside the George, 1920/1. Pictured left to right are: Sparty Glithero, Alf Fellows, Sam Fellows, Sid Freer, Basil Binder, 'Wan' Fillons, John Chambers, Bert Spriggs, Albert Freeman, Tom Fellows and Ted Fellows.

Weldon: Weldon cricket team, 1891, the year they beat Corby. Dr Arthur Stokes, in the jacket, who stands centre, was the top scorer, with just fifteen! Dr Stokes was also an excellent photographer, recording local life.

Weldon: John Preston, landlord of The King's Arms. He is seen here outside one of the entrances to the inn and his name is just discernible on the wooden sign above the door.

Weldon: Kettering Road (formerly Stanion Road), c. 1905. The stretch of road further on to the right is known as Haunt Hill, so-named because of ghost stories attached to the nearby seventeenth-century house (Haunt Hill House). Corby Road is in the background.

Weldon: three of the menservants working for the Rev Finch Hatton at Weldon rectory, *c.* 1915.

Weldon: Amy Stokes, younger daughter of the village doctor, in her pony and trap, outside the family home, Cheyne House, in the High Street. She later married, becoming Amy Wignal, and whilst living in Caldecott, wrote a book about her early years in Weldon.

Weldon: the Queen's Silver Jubilee celebrations, 1977. Some of the merrymakers are seen here in 'fancy dress' walking along Chapel Road to the school playing fields for the children's entertainment programme of events.

Weldon: Mrs M.Griffiths, wife of the rector, cutting the Silver Jubilee cake at the village hall as part of a special tea party at the end of the festivities, for senior citizens.

Gretton: the junction of Station Road with the High Street, *c.* 1925. Another part of the green can be seen, with two public houses which no longer exist: the thatched building on the left is The Fox, and the large house on the right, with the car outside, is The White Hart. The wooden building in the centre was a shop for the baker, Mr Chappell, whose house stands behind.

Gretton: the stocks and whipping post on the green, *c.* 1900. These were renovated during 1996 and are now surrounded by protective railings. The old Gretton Stores can be seen in the background.

Gretton: West Wells, Arnhill Road, 1905. The children are grouped around springs and wells and behind them stands a rare oil-lit lamp. Water was fed into a cistern inside the small building by the railings where the village fire engine was stored.

Gretton: Station Road, looking towards the railway, 1950s. What appears to be a door in the thatched house was in fact a passageway which led to the post office inside, on the right. A short time before this picture was taken, a group of cottages known as Sunnybank had stood on the opposite side of the road.

Gretton: High Street, c. 1955, with the Blue Bell pub on the right.

East Carlton: East Carlton Countryside Park, 1984. The Hall in the background originally belonged to the Palmer family, lords of the manor for many centuries. It was used by Stewarts and Lloyds during the Second World War as offices, and after the war as accommodation for trainee managers and guests. The grounds belonging to the Hall were later opened by Corby District Council for public enjoyment. Relics from the former steel works are on show around the park, some of which can be seen in the foreground.

East Carlton: the stable block of East Carlton Hall before it was converted into the Steel Heritage Centre, where displays and artefacts, documenting the history of the iron and steel industry in the area, can now be seen by the public – a fitting tribute to an important bygone age.

Acknowledgements

I would like to thank Corby Borough Council, British Steel plc,
Northamptonshire Record Office, Bob Mears, Dennis Taylor, Bob Binley,
Bill Boon, Janine Urquhart, Brenda Sismey, Dick Perrell, Danny MacDougall,
Iris Wynn and all those individuals who loaned photographs
from their treasured family albums or collections.
Without their assistance the birth of this book would not have been possible.
All attempts have been made to contact any copyright holders,
and apologies are offered if any such ownership has not been acknowledged.